ALFRED GUITAR METHOD

MW00999325

Contents

WHAT YOU SHOULD KNOW
BEFORE STARTING THIS BOOK 2
KEY OF C MAJOR 3
Rakes of Mallow 4
Home on the Range 5
TUNES THAT TEACH TECHNIC NO. 1 6
Variation on Little Brown Jug 6
Variation on Jim Crack Corn 6
BASS SOLOS WITH CHORD ACCOMPANIMENT 7
Meet Me in St. Louis, Louis 7
KEY OF G MAJOR 8
Tiritomba 8
The Old Chisholm Trail (duet) 9
Simple Gifts (duet) 9
This Land Is Your Land (duet) 10
TUNES THAT TEACH TECHNIC NO. 2 11
Margarita 11
Shortnin' Bread 11
Red River Valley (duet) 12
America (duet) 12
SYNCOPATION 13
The Entertainer (duet) 14
KEY OF A MINOR 16
Waves of the Danube 17
⁶⁄₈ TIME 18
Drink to Me Only with Thine Eyes 18
C.C. Rider 18
TUNES THAT TEACH TECHNIC NO. 3 19
For He's a Jolly Good Fellow 19
Funiculi, Funicula 19
The Irish Washerwoman 19
BASS-CHORD ACCOMPANIMENT: KEY OF C 20
The Yellow Rose of Texas (duet) 21
BASS-CHORD ACCOMPANIMENT: KEY OF G 22
Oh! Susanna (duet) 23

THE KEY OF D MAJOR 24
TUNES THAT TEACH TECHNIC NO. 4 25
Two Etudes in D 25
Joy to the World 25
Marines' Hymn (duet) 26
THE DOTTED 8TH & 16TH NOTE RHYTHM 27
Toreador Song (from Carmen) 27
Straight Jig 28
Worried Man Blues 28
Boogie Blues 28
Careless Love (duet) 29
ALTERNATING BASS NOTES 30
I Ride an Old Paint 31
ALTERNATING BASS NOTES IN THE KEY OF G 32
Mary Ann (duet) 33
TRIPLETS 34
Triumphal March (from Aida) 34
Beautiful Dreamer 35
Sweet Genevieve 35
Spanish Triplets 35
KEY OF E MINOR 36
Etude in E Minor 37
Joshua Fit the Battle 37
KEY OF F MAJOR 38
The Water Is Wide 39
Alphabet Song (Theme and Variation) 39
ALTERNATING BASS NOTES IN THE KEY OF F 40
Oh, My Darling Clementine (duet) 41
Shave and a Haircut 41
The Liberty Bell (duet) 42
Alexander's Ragtime Band (solo or duet) 44
St. Louis Blues (duet) 46
Guitar Boogie 48

Alfred Music
P.O. Box 10003
Van Nuys, CA 91410-0003
alfred.com

Third Edition
Copyright © MCMLIX, MCMXCII, MMVII, MMXV by Alfred Music
All rights reserved. Printed in USA.

Book & Online Audio
ISBN-10: 1-4706-5977-8
ISBN-13: 978-1-4706-5977-6

Book, DVD & Online Audio/Video/Software
ISBN-10: 1-4706-2978-X
ISBN-13: 978-1-4706-2978-6

Front cover guitar photos: Guitar courtesy of Taylor Guitars • Guitarist photo by Jeff Oshiro
Back cover photo models: Luis Cabezas from The Dollyrots (middle right), thedollyrots.com
Back cover photos: Top, and center right: Kevin Estrada • Middle left: © shutterstock.com / Elnur sitting guitarist Bottom: © iStockphoto.com / Nathan McClunie

 Alfred Cares. Contents printed on environmentally responsible paper.

What You Should Know
Before Starting This Book

If you have completed Book 1 of *Alfred's Basic Guitar Method*, you will know the following about playing the guitar. If, however, you know the notes, rhythms, and musical terms on this page (see below), but want to increase your skills and knowledge of scales, chords, and chord accompaniments in the keys of C major, A minor, G major, E minor, D major, and F major, then this book is for you.

All the notes in the 1st position including sharps and flats:

The basic rhythms, including the following:

You should know four basic chords, C, G, G7, and D7, in their four-string forms. These will be reviewed where appropriate.

You should also understand such miscellaneous (but important) terms as pickups, tempo signs (Andante, Moderato, Allegro), bass/chord accompaniments, dynamics (p mf f ff), crescendo (⎯⎯⎯⎯⎯⎯) and decrescendo (⎯⎯⎯⎯⎯⎯), key signatures in C (no sharps or flats), G (one sharp), and F (one flat), and the meaning of *D.S. al Fine* (*dal segno*, go back to the sign 𝄋 and play through to the word *Fine*).

Key of C Major

C MAJOR SCALE Track 2

Three Chords in C

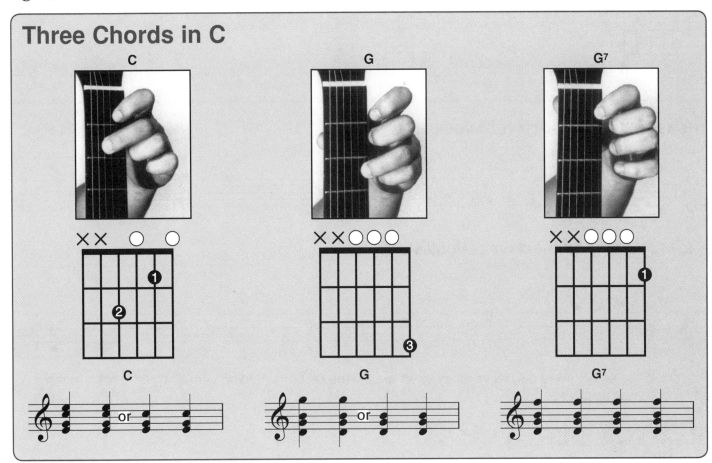

In the diagrams above and throughout this book, the black dots show where to place the fingers and the number inside each dot indicates which finger to use. An open string, meaning one that is played but not fingered, will not have a dot, but will have an "o" above it. A string with an "x" above it means that string is not to be played.

ACCOMPANIMENT IN C MAJOR Track 3

USE DOWN-STROKES ONLY

* When introduced, chord names are written above the chords so the student may learn the notes of the chord as well as its name.

4

The C major scale can be extended to a full two octaves by adding high A, high B, and high C.

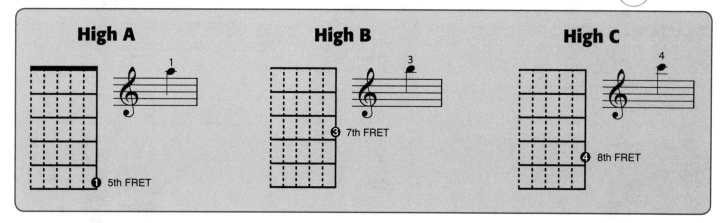

THE ASCENDING TWO-OCTAVE C MAJOR SCALE

SHIFT THE HAND UP THE NECK

THE DESCENDING TWO-OCTAVE C MAJOR SCALE

SHIFT DOWN THE NECK

Practice these scales every day. Make every effort to play the sections marked with a  as smoothly as possible.

RAKES OF MALLOW

Track 5

Allegro

TEACHER: C

Irish fiddle tune

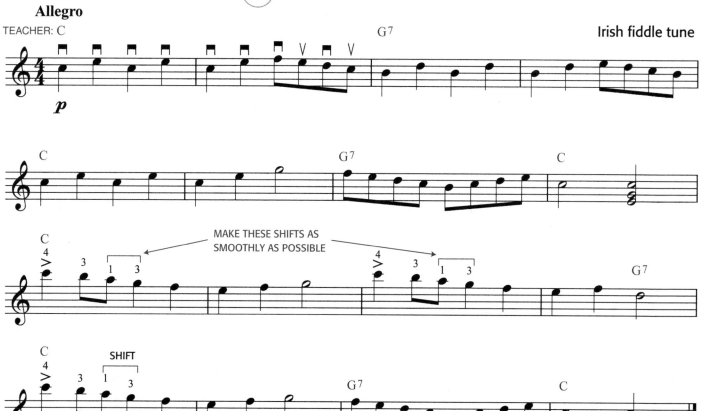

F minor is a new chord that requires putting your 1st finger down across three strings. Press hard near (but not on) the 1st fret.

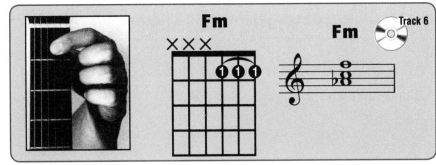

HOME ON THE RANGE

Track 7

The melody may be sung or played.

American cowboy song

* A wavy line in front of a chord ⦃ means to run the pick across the strings more slowly to obtain a rippling, harp-like sound.
The technical name for this effect is the Italian word *arpeggiando*, usually abbreviated *arp.*

Tunes that Teach Technic No. 1

VARIATION ON LITTLE BROWN JUG  Track 8

For developing technic in repeated notes.

VARIATION ON JIM CRACK CORN Track 9

Combining scale passages and chords.

* The symbol 𝄵 means *cut time*, indicating that the time value is cut in half; half notes receive 1 beat, quarter notes receive ½ beat, etc.

Bass Solos with Chord Accompaniment

When bass solos are played with chord accompaniment, the solo part is written with the stems descending, and the chords with the stems ascending.

In the example below, the bass solo begins on the first beat and is held for three beats; the quarter rest shows that the chord accompaniment begins on the second beat.

MEET ME IN ST. LOUIS, LOUIS Track 10

A. B. Sterling
and Kerry Mills

Key of G Major

The key signature of one sharp indicates the key of G major. Each F is played as F♯ unless otherwise indicated by a natural sign.

G MAJOR SCALE Track 11

The Three Principal Chords in G

The three *principal,* or most commonly used, chords in any key are built on the first, fourth, and fifth notes of the scale. The chord built on the fifth note usually adds a seventh tone to it. The chords are known as 1, 4, 5(7) chords and are notated by Roman numerals: I, IV, V7. The three principal chords in the key of G are G, C, and D7.

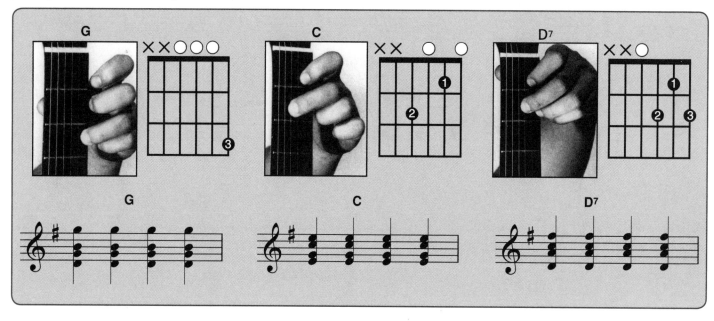

TIRITOMBA Track 12

First learn the melody, which is in the key of G and makes use of many repeated notes. Then, have your teacher or a friend play the melody while you strum the chords, four to each measure.

THE OLD CHISHOLM TRAIL (DUET)

Track 13

Student to learn both parts. Then play as a duet with your teacher or a friend. Finally, sing the melody (top staff) while playing the accompaniment (bottom staff).

* Remember: F is played F♯ in the key of G.

SIMPLE GIFTS (DUET)

Track 14

THIS LAND IS YOUR LAND (DUET)

Track 15

Student to learn both parts.

Woody Guthrie

This land is your land,____ this land is my land,____

____ from Cal - i - for - nia____ to the New York is - land,____

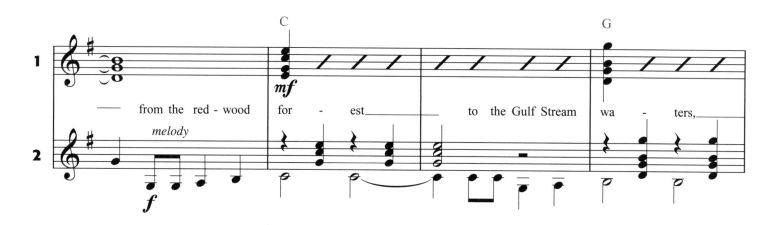

____ from the red - wood for - est____ to the Gulf Stream wa - ters,

this land was made for you and me.____

Tunes That Teach Technic No. 2

MARGARITA  Track 17

Study in 3rds.

March tempo

SHORTNIN' BREAD  Track 18

For developing fluency in skips.

Moderato

12

RED RIVER VALLEY (DUET)

Track 19

Moderato

AMERICA (DUET)

Track 20

Andante

Syncopation Track 21

Syncopation is the name given to a musical effect in which a note is *anticipated*, meaning it is played before its expected beat. For example, the rhythm below is not syncopated—each quarter note falls in the expected place, *on the beat*.

The example below uses syncopation. The third quarter note is played on the "&" of the second beat rather than on its expected place on the third beat.

For best results, count carefully and *accent* >
(play a little louder) all syncopated notes.

The following syncopations occur in the next tune you will learn.
Practice them carefully before attempting "The Entertainer" on the next page.

Basic rhythm:

1st variation:

2nd variation:

3rd variation:

Another syncopation:

Can be thought of as:

Still another:

Combined:

THE ENTERTAINER (DUET)

Track 22

The first music to make extensive use of syncopation was called *ragtime*. It became very popular around the turn of the 20th century. This ragtime composition was used as the main theme for the movie *The Sting*.

Student to learn both parts.

Scott Joplin

REPEAT SIGN

Go back to repeat sign.   Go on to the next line.

Go back to repeat sign.   End.

Key of A Minor Track 23

For every major key, there is a minor key with the same key signature called the *relative minor key*. The keys of A minor and C major are relative keys becuase they have the same key signature (no sharps, no flats). The relative minor scale is built on the 6th tone of the major scale. Chords are built on the harmonic minor scale, which has its 7th step *augmented* (raised a half step).

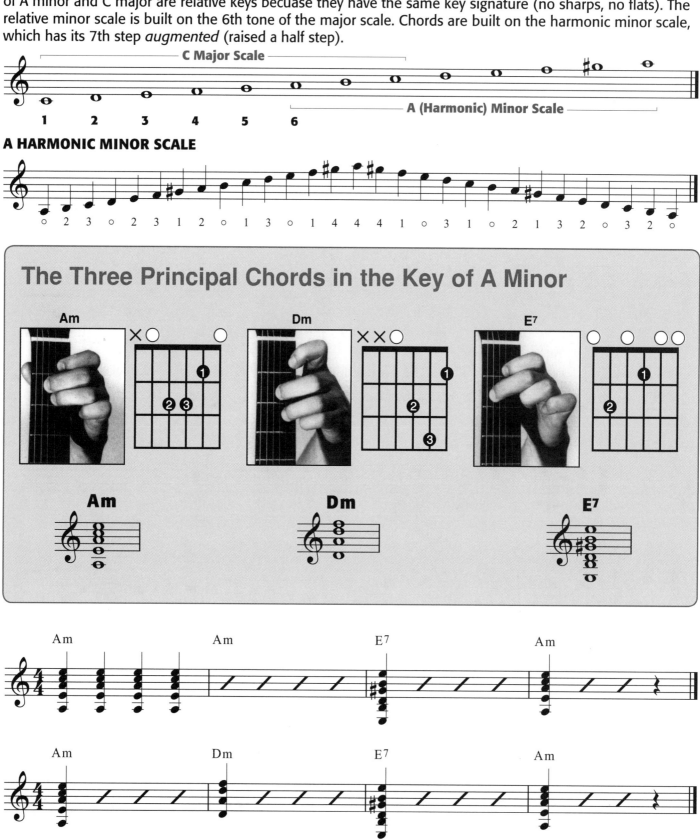

WAVES OF THE DANUBE (KEY OF A MINOR) Track 24

This melody by Romanian composer Ion Ivanovici is frequently played at anniversary celebrations.

* *D.C.* means go back to the beginning. *D.C. al Coda* means play from the beginning to the ⊕, then skip directly
  to the *coda* (the last two measures).
** A *Coda* is an added ending.

$\frac{6}{8}$ Time

The time signature $\frac{6}{8}$ = six beats in each measure
$\frac{6}{8}$ = eighth note gets one beat

COUNT: 1 2 3 4 5 6

NOTE AND REST VALUES IN $\frac{6}{8}$

1 2 3 4 5 6   1 2 3 4 5 6   1 2 3 4 5 6   1 2 3 4 5 6   1 2 3 4 5 6

DRINK TO ME ONLY WITH THINE EYES

Track 25

Andante

TEACHER: C   G7   C G7 C G7 C G7   C   F G7   1. C   2. C

mp (moderately soft)

COUNT: 1 2 3 4 5 6

C   F   C   G7

C   G7   C G7 C G7 C G7   C   F G7   C

C. C. RIDER

Track 26

Moderate Blues ♩. = 72

G   C   G   D7   G

C   G

G7   D7   C

G   C   G   D7   G

Tunes That Teach Technic No. 3

FOR HE'S A JOLLY GOOD FELLOW — Track 27

Allegro

D.S. %̸ al Fine*

* Go back to the sign %̸ and play to the Fine.

FUNICULI, FUNICULA — Track 28

Allegro

THE IRISH WASHERWOMAN — Track 29

Irish folk tune

Allegro

COUNT: (1 2 3 4) 5 6

KEEP 3rd FINGER DOWN

Bass-Chord Accompaniment: Key of C

Chord accompaniment is considerably improved by replacing the first chord of each measure with a bass note. The simplest bass note is the *root* (the letter name) of the chord, or simply the bass note (BN). The three principal chords in the key of C are C, F, and G7.

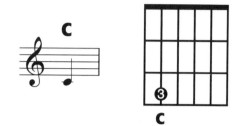

With the C (I) chord, play the bass note C.

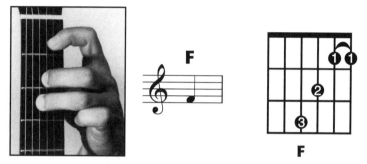

With the F (IV) chord, play the bass note F.

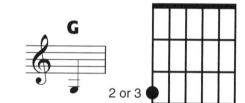

With the G or G7 (V7) chord, play the bass note G.

Bass–Chord–Chord–Chord

Track 30

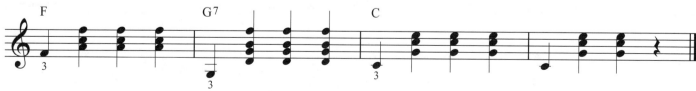

* On certain occasions, it is preferable to use the thumb for bass notes on the low E string when followed by a chord. Try both fingerings and use the one that is easier for you.

THE YELLOW ROSE OF TEXAS (DUET)

Moderato

She's my Rose-bud, she's my Dar-lin'! My love is sweet and true! I

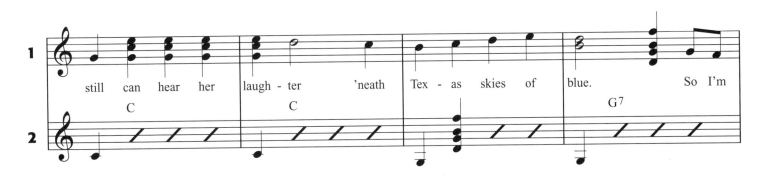

still can hear her laugh-ter 'neath Tex-as skies of blue. So I'm

get-tin' set to hur-ry back and I know there she'll be, my sweet

Yel-low Rose of Tex-as there a-wait-in' faith-ful-ly.

Bass-Chord Accompaniment: Key of G

As shown on page 8, the three principal chords in the key of G are G, C, and D7:

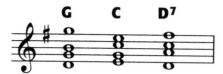

THE THREE PRINCIPAL CHORDS WITH THE ROOT OR BASS NOTE

The *root* of a chord is the note that names it. For example, the root of a G chord is the note G; the root of a D7 chord is D and so on.

OH! SUSANNA (DUET)

Stephen Foster

The Key of D Major

The key signature of two sharps indicates the key of D major. Each F is played as F♯ and each C is played as C♯ unless otherwise indicated by a natural sign. To play the two-octave D major scale, you'll need two new notes on the 1st string: high C♯ (1st string, 9th fret) and high D (1st string, 10th fret).

When learning the two-octave D major scale below, follow the fingering carefully. Like all scales, this one should be practiced daily.

D MAJOR SCALE · Track 36

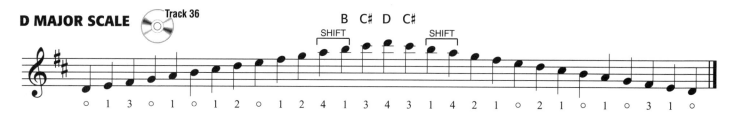

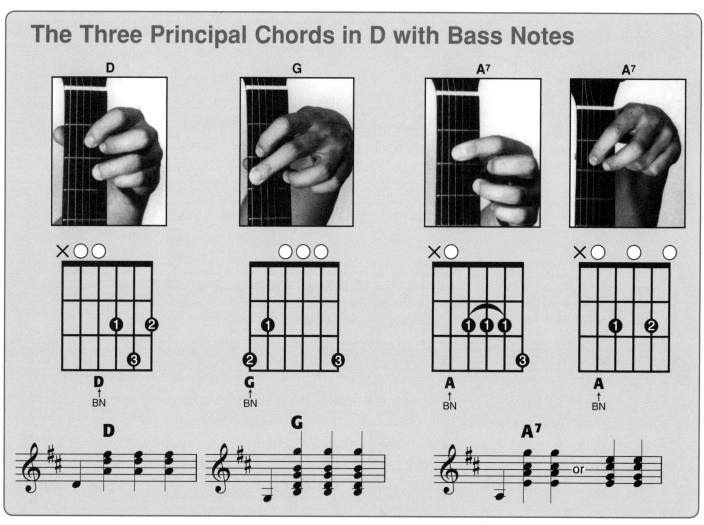

The Three Principal Chords in D with Bass Notes

ACCOMPANIMENT IN **D MAJOR** · Track 37

Tunes That Teach Technic No. 4

TWO ETUDES IN D
Track 38

1.

2.

JOY TO THE WORLD
Track 39

The student should learn both the melody and the accompanying chords of this Christmas favorite.

Majestically

Marines' Hymn (DUET)

Track 40

March tempo

The Dotted 8th & 16th Note Rhythm

Like 8th notes, dotted 8ths and 16ths are played two to each beat. But unlike 8th notes (which are played evenly) dotted 8ths and 16ths are played *unevenly*: long, short, long, short.

Compare the following:

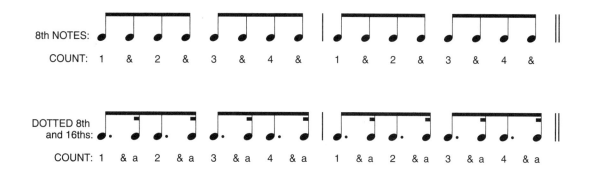

An easy way to remember the sound of dotted 8ths and 16ths is to say the words:

"hump - ty dump - ty hump - ty dump - ty"

The dotted 8th and 16th note rhythm is very common in all kinds of music, but especially classical, folk, country, and blues. Here are examples of each to practice.

TOREADOR SONG Track 41

(FROM *CARMEN*)

George Bizet

28

Student to play melody and chords for all songs on this page.

The dotted 8th and 16th note rhythm can be combined with bass-chord style to create a type of accompaniment called the *shuffle beat*. Keep in mind the "hump-ty dump-ty" rhythm of the accompaniment, and use down-picks and up-picks to accomplish it.

CARELESS LOVE (DUET) — Track 45

Traditional blues

* ⅞ means to repeat previous measure.

Alternating Bass Notes

An *alternate bass note* is any note except the root of the chord (usually the 5th note of the scale).

Alternate bass notes are used to enrich the accompaniment when the harmony remains the same for several consecutive measures.

This accompaniment is good:

But this is better:

Alternating Bass Notes in the Key of C

Complete forms of the C and G7 chords are shown here. If the stretches can be handled, their use is preferred when playing accompaniment. Finger the complete chord at the beginning of the measure and hold it until the chord changes.

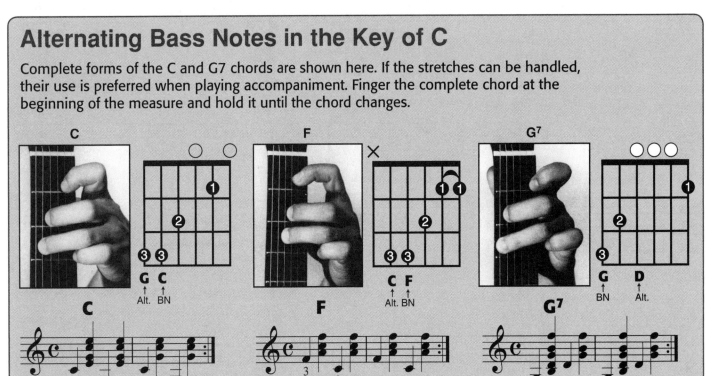

ACCOMPANIMENT IN C MAJOR   Track 46

I RIDE AN OLD PAINT (DUET)

 Track 47

* *Pull-off:* Do not pick the second note. Pull the 2nd finger off the string so that the open G note sounds.

Alternating Bass Notes in the Key of G

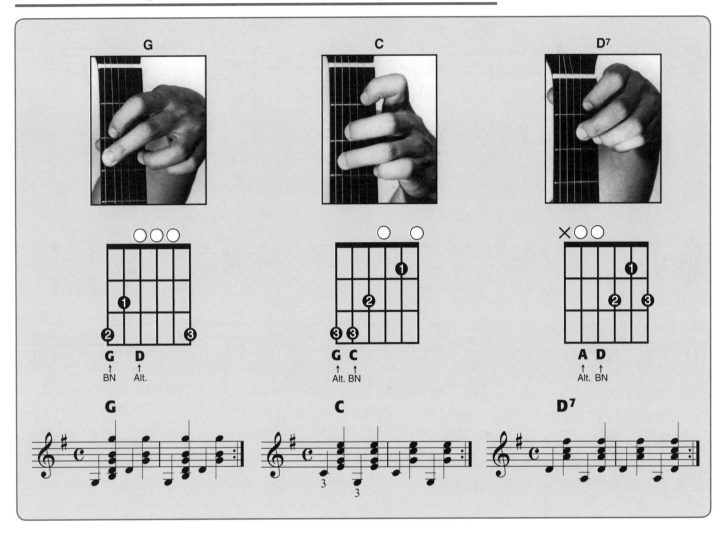

Track 48

ACCOMPANIMENT IN G MAJOR

MARY ANN (DUET)

Track 49

Allegro

Triplets  Track 50

When three notes are grouped together with the figure "3" above or below them, the group is called a *triplet*. The three notes then have the same value as is ordinarily given to two of the notes. In $\frac{3}{4}$ or $\frac{4}{4}$ time, two eighth notes get one count, so an eighth note triplet will also get one count.

In the following exercise, play the three notes of each triplet on one count.

TRIUMPHAL MARCH  Track 51

(FROM *AIDA*)

Maestoso (Majestically)

Giuseppe Verdi

* *D.C. al Fine* means go back to the beginning and play to the *fine* (the end).

BEAUTIFUL DREAMER  Track 52

Andante

Stephen Foster

SWEET GENEVIEVE Track 53

Andante

PLAY: G7 C / F G7 / / G7 / / C / /

SING: Oh, Gen - e - vieve, sweet Gen - e - vieve, the days may come, the days may go, but

C / / F / / C / / G7 C

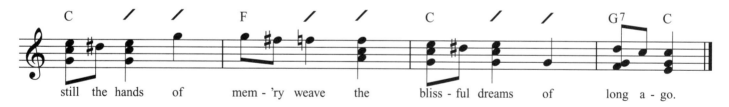

still the hands of mem - 'ry weave the bliss - ful dreams of long a - go.

SPANISH TRIPLETS Track 54

Allegro

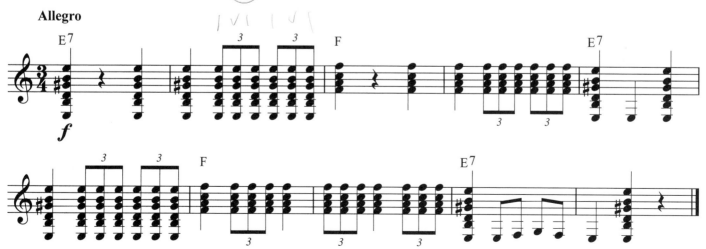

Key of E Minor 🎵 Track 55

E minor and G major are relative keys because they both have the key signature
of one sharp (F♯) Like the A minor scale, the E minor scale is built on the 6th tone
of the relative (G) major.

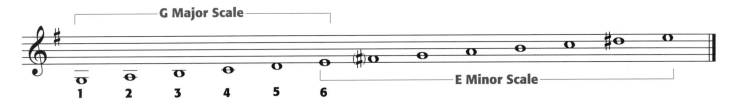

E HARMONIC MINOR SCALE

The Three Principal Chords in the Key of E Minor

Em   Am   B7

E B   A E   B D♯
BN Alt.   BN Alt.   BN Alt.

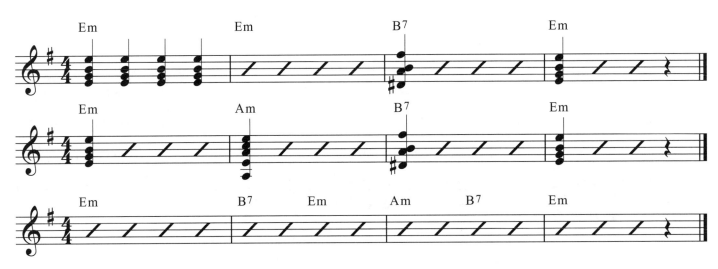

ETUDE IN E MINOR Track 56

COUNT: 1 & 2 & 3 &   4   &

JOSHUA FIT THE BATTLE Track 57

Learn the melody and chords.

Moderately, with a beat

Gospel tune

Josh - ua fit the bat - tle of___ Jer - i - cho,___ Jer - i - cho,___

Jer - i - cho;___ Josh - ua fit the bat - tle of___ Jer - i - cho___ and the

1.

2. *Fine*

walls came tum - blin' down. (That morn - in')___ down.

You may talk a - bout your King of Gid - e - on, you may

talk a - bout your man of Saul, but there's none like good old

D.C. al Fine *

Josh - u - a___ at the bat - tle of Jer - i - cho.

* Remember to play from the beginning, then skip the 1st ending and end with the 2nd ending.

Key of F Major

The key signature of one flat indicates the key of F major. All B's are played as B♭ unless otherwise indicated by a natural sign.

F MAJOR SCALE Track 58

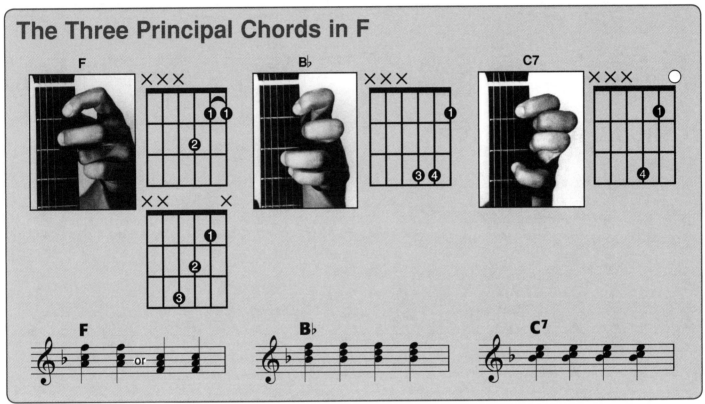

ACCOMPANIMENT IN F MAJOR Track 59

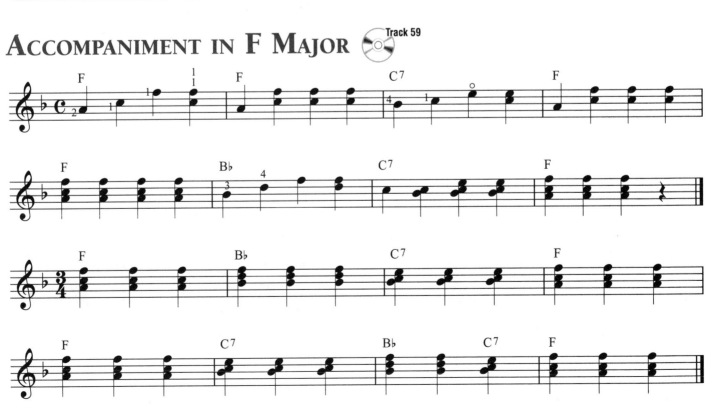

THE WATER IS WIDE   Track 60

Slowly

ALPHABET SONG (THEME AND VARIATION)   Track 61

Variation

LEARN EACH OCTAVE SEPARATELY

Alternating Bass Notes in the Key of F

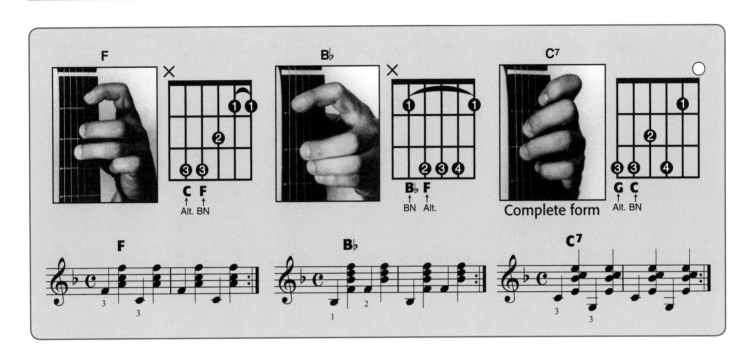

ACCOMPANIMENT IN F MAJOR — Track 62

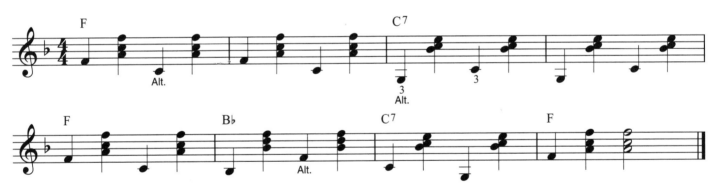

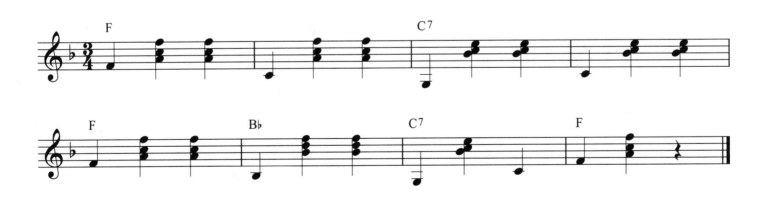

OH, MY DARLING CLEMENTINE (DUET)

Track 63

Moderato

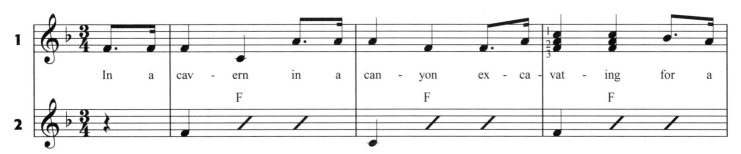

In a cav - ern in a can - yon ex - ca - vat - ing for a

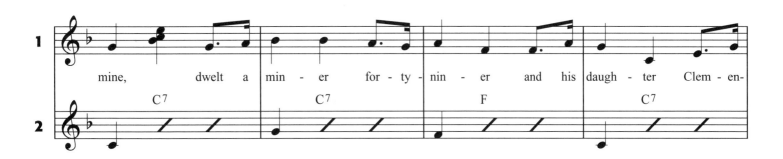

mine, dwelt a min - er for - ty - nin - er and his daugh - ter Clem - en -

tine. Oh my dar - ling, oh my dar - ling, oh my dar - ling Clem - en -

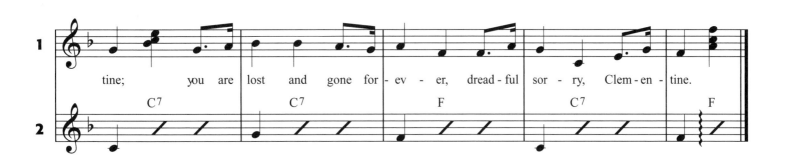

tine; you are lost and gone for - ev - er, dread - ful sor - ry, Clem - en - tine.

SHAVE AND A HAIRCUT

Track 64

Briskly

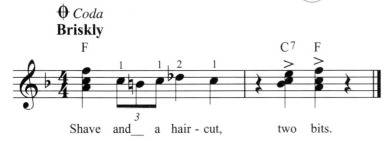

Shave and a hair - cut, two bits.

42

THE LIBERTY BELL (DUET)

Before attempting this famous march by John Philip Sousa, you may want to review the discussion of $\frac{6}{8}$ time on page 18.

John Philip Sousa

Brisk march tempo

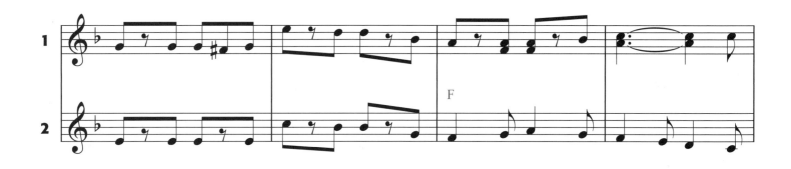

* The *marcato* accent (∧ or ∨) is a stressed accent.

ALEXANDER'S RAGTIME BAND (SOLO OR DUET)

Track 66

With a beat

Irving Berlin

St. Louis Blues (DUET)

Moderate blues tempo

W. C. Handy

GUITAR BOOGIE Track 68

This is perhaps the most famous guitar solo ever recorded. It's definitely worth the extra effort you may have to make to master it.

Moderate boogie tempo

Arthur Smith